Voice Production and Speech

COMPANION CASSETTE

A **C30 cassette** is available which contains recording of possible interpretations of some of the exercises in *Speech Practice* and *Voice Production and Speech*. The recordings were made by the author of the two books, Greta Colson, with a group of her students at the New College of Speech and Drama, London, where she is Principal Lecturer.

Speech Practice
Greta Colson

Side one covers some of the exercises in this book, namely: 1, 8, 16, 23, 24, 34, 35, 42, 43, 48, 53, 82, 92, 135, 159.

Voice Production and Speech
Greta Colson

Side two covers the additional exercises listed under the Appendix on page 81 of this book. The exercises demonstrated are: 3, 4, 5, 7, 8, 10, 11, 12 (two interpretations) and 13 (parts i, ii, iii, iv, v, vi).

VOICE PRODUCTION AND SPEECH

by

GRETA COLSON

Principal Lecturer in charge of Voice, Middlesex Polytechnic
Formerly Professor, Royal Academy of Music—Speech and Drama Faculty
Examiner for:
Licentiate of Royal Academy of Music
Associated Board of Royal Schools of Music
University of London, Diploma in Speech and Drama
Central School of Speech and Drama
Adjudicator for:
Federation of Music Festivals (Speech and Drama)
F.R.S.A.M.D., F.N.C.S.D., C.S.S.D., L.R.A.M., L.G.S.M., I.P.A. Certificate

PITMAN

PITMAN PUBLISHING LIMITED
39 Parker Street, London WC2B 5PB

Associated Companies
Copp Clark Pitman Ltd, Toronto
Fearon Pitman Publishers Inc, San Francisco
Pitman Publishing New Zealand Ltd, Wellington
Pitman Publishing Pty Ltd, Melbourne

© Greta Colson 1963, 1973

Second edition (under Pitman imprint) 1973
First paperback edition 1973
Reprinted 1974, 1977, 1979

Printed and bound in Great Britain
at The Pitman Press, Bath

ISBN 0 273 31769 5

PREFACE

THE terms used in Voice Theory and Speech Training are inherited from singing teachers, borrowed from physics, adapted from phonetics, dictated by physiology and born in the imagination of speech teachers. Contemporary advances in technical knowledge of the subject have added further complications.

It is not surprising that writers on the subject exhibit considerable inconsistency both in the particular terms they employ and in the meanings they attach to these. For even the enlightened teacher the task of guiding students through this labyrinth is an exacting one.

A clear presentation of the language used in teaching speech and voice is therefore of primary concern and this book is intended to provide an introductory course for students and others interested in the subject.

Thanks are due to Dr. Wilfred Barlow for help on posture problems and to John Colson for advice on phonological aspects.

My thanks are also due to the following for allowing their work to be reproduced:

George MacBeth and Macmillan's for the *Clapping Poem* on page 81

David Bell and Angela Konrad for *Down by the Mersey* on page 82

David Bell for *Call it Aloud* on page 82 and *The Gale* on page 82

Peter Kay for the song on page 83

Bob Cobbing for the poems on pages 84-7

CONTENTS

PART IV: WORD

ILLUSTRATIONS

KEY WORDS FOR VOWEL SOUNDS

PHONETIC symbols are not used in this book. The following key words, however, have been provided. The operative sound is in italics in each instance.

PURE VOWELS	DIPHTHONGS
H*EE*D	H*ERE*
H*I*D	H*ARE*
H*EA*D	H*OA*R
H*A*D	T*OU*R
H*EAR*D	H*AY*
*A*BOUT	H*IGH*
H*U*T	H*OW*
H*AR*D	H*OY*
H*O*CK	H*OE*
H*AW*K	
H*OO*K	
H*OO*T	

INTRODUCTION

THIS book is divided into sections under the following headings:

PART I: BREATH

PART II: NOTE

PART III: TONE

PART IV: WORD

These four stages in the production of voice and speech may be tabulated as shown below.

(This plan must be read from the bottom upwards: it is put in this way in accordance with the position of the anatomical features involved. The whole physical process is initiated by the BREATH, which is largely controlled by the action of the diaphragm, and culminates in the WORD, which is formed in the front of the mouth.)

PHONOLOGY	ANATOMY	PHYSICS	FUNCTION	CONTROL
4. WORD	Speech Organs	Particular Resonance	Particular Quality	(a) Ear (b) Muscular Sensation
3. TONE	Nose Mouth Neck	General Resonance	General Quality	(a) Ear (b) Muscular Sensation
2. NOTE	Vocal Folds	Vibrator (Frequency)	Pitch	Ear, in conjunction with mental image of sound required
1. BREATH	Lungs	Excitor (Amplitude)	Capacity and Control	Diaphragm in association with abdominal muscles and ribs operated by intercostal muscles

PART I: BREATH

SUMMARY

Breath enters and leaves the body in accordance with the alternate increase and decrease of the size of the chest (and hence of the size of the lungs, which expand and contract according to the size of the chest itself). These changes in the size of the chest are brought about by muscular contraction and relaxation. It is the *contraction* of the intercostal muscles which moves the ribs upwards and outwards, and the *contraction* of the muscle fibres of the diaphragm which moves its central tendon downwards and makes it less dome-shaped. Thus the size of the chest is increased (*a*) laterally and (*b*) vertically; in both cases by an active muscular contraction. Breathing out is the result of relaxation of the muscles but in speech it must be controlled relaxation. In vocalization the outgoing breath interacts with the vibrating vocal folds. These impart to it the waves which after passing through the resonator are heard by the ear of the listener as "sound".

THE STRUCTURE OF THE CHEST (OR THORAX)

(*A*) *BONE* forms a cage which protects the upper part of the body. The SPINE, or backbone, is made up of a series of vertebrae. From the twelve dorsal vertebrae pairs of ribs pass down and round rising in the front to make a complete closure with the sternum.

Feel these on your own spine. Trace the ribs round. Feel the sweep of each rib.

13

THE BONES OF THE THORAX

Counting from the top:

The first seven pairs of ribs join with the sternum.

The next three pairs join with the seventh.

Two pairs are floating (they are free at the front end).

Place your hand on your waist at the side. The free ends are just above it.

Elasticity is given because the join between bone and bone (i.e. rib and sternum) is completed with cartilage, which is softer than bone.

(B) *MUSCLE* enables bone to move. A muscle can move in two ways only. It can contract (and so grow shorter, bringing bone towards bone) and it can cease to contract and so return to its original position.

Muscle can be seen when raw meat is cut. "A muscle" consists of many muscle fibres and these fibres form a tough, solid sheet.

Muscles begin at one stable bone position (point of origin) and end at a second bone (point of insertion).

The Breathing Muscles

Each rib is raised towards the one above, extending the rib cage and so making the chest larger. The muscles that contract to raise the ribs are the Intercostals (between ribs). There are two sets of intercostals; the Internal and External.

The central and lower ribs have a large movement. They are relatively free and have a different shape from that of the upper ribs. This makes them move Outwards as well as upwards when one rib is raised towards the one above.

There is a strong muscle which divides the thorax and the abdomen. It is the Diaphragm. The muscle fibres originate at the lower edge of the ribs, the point of the sternum and the vertebrae. They then rise in a dome shape and insert into a flat, trefoil shaped central tendon. This central tendon cannot contract, so it is a stable factor and is moved only by the contraction of the muscle fibres of the diaphragm.

During repose the rib movement is slight. Breath is taken mainly by the diaphragm, which descends and so the chest space is made larger. The movement is a gentle one and the diaphragm descends an inch to an inch and a half.

When more breath is needed the rib movement is increased. This pulls the edges of the diaphragm outwards and reduces the domed shape as shown below.

You can feel these muscles between your ribs making the rib wall solid. Now feel the lower ribs at the back where there should be an outward and upward movement. After this place your hands on the ribs just below the shoulders in front where the movement can be felt but is slight because the ribs have less freedom. When you breathe the shoulders should ride easily and the whole chest should be filled. The shoulders should never be rigid.

The diaphragm cannot be felt but the effect of its rise and fall can be felt if you place your hand on the arch between the ribs in front (epigastrium). When the diaphragm descends the epigastrium moves outwards; it moves back to its original position as the diaphragm ascends.

DIAGRAM OF THE DIAPHRAGM

The dotted line shows the descent of the central tendon on the outward and upward movement of the ribs.

PASSAGE OF THE BREATH

The breath enters through the

MOUTH or NOSE (or both).
It passes down through the

PHARYNX (or neck) and has a free passage through the

LARYNX into the

TRACHEA. This is the windpipe and leads from the larynx in the neck into the thorax. It subdivides into two

BRONCHI which enter the two lungs, branch and there subdivide into minute tubes ending in air-sacs in the

LUNGS. These with the heart fill the thoracic cavity. The right lung has an upper, middle and lower lobe. The left an upper and lower. The lungs are conical in shape and follow the shape of the inside of the thorax. When the chest is enlarged the lungs follow its new shape.

Realization that the lungs are made up of separate lobes may make taking a full breath an easier process.

THE ORDER OF THE BREATHING PROCESS

Breathing is primarily for supplying oxygen to the blood. When the amount of carbon dioxide in the blood stream reaches a certain tension the breathing muscles are stimulated into contracting.

1. The muscles contract enlarging the chest cavity and
2. The breath passes into the lungs equalizing the pressure between the air in the lungs and the air outside.
3. The muscles cease to contract and the chest cavity returns to its original size and
4. The breath passes out as the size of the lungs is reduced, so equalizing the pressure between the air in the lungs and the air outside.

During gentle breathing only about one-tenth of the total amount of air in the lungs passes in and out. This is known as TIDAL AIR. The amount of tidal air can be considerably increased at will but nearly half the air always remains in the lungs and is known as RESIDUAL AIR. About a quarter remains even after very forceful breathing out.

Breath can be given more capacity and control by:

1. RIB SWING. The ribs are moved outwards and upwards and the diaphragm descends so enlarging the chest in circumference and length. The continued alternation between contraction and relaxation of the muscles gives a rhythmical rise and fall to the ribs.

Drop your arms to the side. Keep your arms easy and turn the hands placing the backs of them on the sixth and seventh ribs. The rib swing can be felt.

2. RIB RESERVE BREATHING. The ribs are extended and held in this position. The diaphragm continues to contract and relax independently. This method ensures plenty of air in the chest throughout the procedure and helps the tone to be steady and secure. The breath can be taken quickly and silently through the mouth. The ribs being raised helps the position of the larynx.

Keep one hand on the ribs and place the other on the abdominal wall in the arch between the ribs. The ribs stay out but the movement of the diaphragm can be felt by the movement of the abdominal muscles forming the body wall in the arch between the ribs. These move out when the breath enters the chest and in when the breath passes out. This is especially clear if you keep your ribs out and then pant gently.

The movement of the upper ABDOMINAL MUSCLES in breathing is antagonistic to that of the diaphragm. As the diaphragm descends on breathing in, the upper abdominal muscles relax allowing the slight forward bulge of the upper abdominal wall. As the diaphragm ascends on breathing out the abdominal muscles contract and the abdominal wall reverts to its previous position.

The word "antagonist" in its technical sense implies co-operation rather then opposition.

BREATHING AND VOCAL PRACTICE

Vocal practice should be undertaken when one is feeling fresh and vitally alive and should not be crammed into the day's activity as a matter of conscience.

POSTURE

The whole body is involved in the production of vocal sound so practice begins with posture. Unfortunately, when man became upright, balancing his weight on the two relatively small triangles of his feet, he immediately increased the tension in his muscles which affected posture and vocal production.

An important muscle area for speakers is found at the back of the neck where muscular contraction tilts back the head, sticks out the chin and impairs the laryngeal functioning. Before speaking with any power, most people contract these muscles. To correct the fault, deliberately relax these muscles. Break the habit by beginning to speak only when you are muscularly ready: rushing into vocalization means encouraging poor usage. Check yourself carefully in a front plus side mirror for the following posture faults.

(a) Placing weight unevenly to left or right.

(b) Pulled in and unevenly positioned shoulders.

(c) Head tilted to right or left; or head pulled back with chin drawn in; or head thrust forward with chin out.

(d) Spine not lengthening: spine curving excessively in lumbar area hollowing back: left or right curves.

(e) A pulled-in thorax: rigidity in this area.

(Refer, too, to past photographs.)

Resolving Posture Difficulties

The following exercises are based on the Alexander Technique.

(a) Supine Position. Follow the directions on page 21.

(b) Monkey Position. Stand with your feet set fairly widely apart. Bend your knees a little keeping feet and knees out. Bring your head, neck and trunk forward in one line until your head is over your feet. This is a good position in which to further the experience of breathing as it exposes the lower back ribs, a vital area. The position is hard on the legs, so when you wish, come up in two stages, first the trunk and head, then straighten the legs. Continue letting energy go up through your body.

(c) Sit, keeping your spine lengthening and coming up from the chair. Do not sink down into it. Do not lean against the back of the chair. Stand by unbending your knees and do not lurch forward. Sail up and have the sensation of continuing to go up. Sit, by reversing the process.

(*d*) Stretch out your arms sideways, ease your shoulders and think them out. Continue to do this taking your time and as the shoulders cease to pull in the arms will elongate.

(*e*) Sit, keeping your length and spreading your shoulders. Then come forward with the lower trunk, hold the position, then go back with the upper trunk appreciating the way the guts lift.

(*f*) Spread the shoulders and then encourage the sensation of the shoulder girdle dropping back over the rib-cage. At the same time think of energy rising up the spine.

(*g*) Keep the length of your body and walk, carried by a movement from the hip joints. Do not let the knees bend or the pelvis come into play.

(*h*) Throughout your body think bone away from bone; let your body energize outwards, do not hug yourself in.

(*i*) Good body usage applies to all human activities not only to specific undertakings.

(*j*) Terminology: LENGTHEN NOT SHORTEN. HEAD: FORWARD AND UP NOT BACK AND DOWN. SPREAD NOT DRAWN IN.

PHYSICAL EXERCISES IN PREPARATION FOR BREATHING

INTRODUCTION

The idea of weight "dropping" from parts of the body, the spreading outwards of all parts, and the energy mounting up the back to the head and fanning out to the shoulders, precedes wide strong general movement.

FEET AND LEGS

The legs are swung freely from the hip, the knees made flexible and the ankles and parts of the foot moved. Energy passes into the feet and up into the body. When standing, the weight should be evenly balanced between the feet and slightly back on the heels; knees must not be tensed, neither may they sag; lightness of movement should be the aim. All foot exercises should be done either in unblocked practice shoes or with bare feet.

THE TRUNK

The waist should be made flexible with various bending and twisting movements. The spine needs special attention; the length and upright stretch of it gives a sensation of rising energy. The small of the back must be easy so that there is no undue hollowing. A valuable exercise is the following:—

Lie with the back on the floor with a book two inches thick supporting the head. Place the heels eighteen inches or so apart and allow the feet to rotate outwards; the arms lie easily by the sides palms downwards. A sense of physical and mental ease should be cultivated.

Keep the knees apart and bend the knees, letting the feet travel along the ground towards the body until they are under the knees. The whole spine should now be straight and moulded to the floor. If there is still a curve in the lumbar region and this part of the spine does not touch the floor do not force it down but bring the knees together and up towards the chin so that the spine is now touching the floor. Now let the legs go back slowly to the previous position, maintaining the contact between the spine and the floor in the lumbar region. Whilst in this position cultivate a sense of the lengthening and widening of the back of the shoulders flat on the floor and the neck projecting well out of and away from the rest of the spine. No movement is needed; just observe the sensation. Let the feet slide outwards again; the curve in the lumbar region will reassert itself. The object of this exercise is to correct excessive lumbar curvature. The sensation of the straight back when the legs are bent should be registered mentally.

Repeat the same exercise but in a vertical position against a wall. Place the feet about eighteen inches apart with the toes pointed out at an angle of forty-five degrees and the heels about two inches from the wall. Let the body move back in one piece from the ankles against the wall. If the posture is correct shoulders and buttocks touch the wall at the same time. Let the knees travel forwards and outwards over the toes so that the body slides down the wall about one foot. The whole spine should now make contact with the wall in the same way as when the knees were bent in the supine position on the floor. If it does not, this is an indication that the habitual poise involves excessive lumbar curvature. Regular practice of this exercise on the floor and then against the wall helps to remedy this. As in the previous exercise when the correct position is achieved the sensation should be registered mentally so that it becomes part of one's body image. As the knees travel forwards and outwards a sensation that the head is remaining up in the air and that the body is lengthening is experienced; the thought should not be of a downward movement. The head must not be allowed to fall back so that it touches the wall. When coming up again the sensation is not one of pressing upwards with the feet or the knees but rather of the head rising effortlessly, as if it were lighter than air, and the rest of the body following. When the body is erect there will of course be some curve in the lumbar region. This is perfectly natural and only excessive curvature is undesirable. A slump in the lumbar region which often occurs in a seated position is equally to be avoided.

SHOULDERS, ARMS AND HANDS

The roll of the shoulders has to be felt well within the body. The shoulders form a cross with the spine and balance on either side of it in a see-saw action. There should be a feeling of the shoulders branching from the spine; the arms should turn out from the shoulder, with elbows out, wrists in, hands out. Arms and hands should be exercised in all possible directions, strong aggressive movements alternating with lyrical, delicate ones.

Particular attention has to be given to the shoulders in breathing. Rigidity must be avoided so that when the lungs fill to a good capacity the shoulders ride easily. There should be no hint of holding them down to prevent them "rising". It is particularly important to refer to this point because of the old trick children have of shrugging the shoulders to emphasize that they have obligingly taken in a breath as requested. A tense upper chest can be caused by over-correcting this fault.

NECK AND HEAD

Great ease is needed in all neck and head exercises. Special attention should be given to the set of the head. The head position begins at the feet and energy rising up through the body balances the head in the way a ball balances on a jet of water. Common faults are drooping shoulders and a poked forward head. The well-positioned column of the neck is a vital point of posture. The head and neck have to be regarded as free and mobile and not as being set in a fixed position. Unless the spine, shoulders and neck are interacting successfully the open throat position needed for good voice production eludes the speaker.

BREATHING EXERCISES

BREATHING EXERCISES SHOULD INCREASE THE CAPACITY OF THE BREATH AND DEVELOP CONTROL OF IT.

There are three points to be remembered:—

(a) There should never be undue physical demand made on anyone during breathing exercises. The aim should be a gradual increase of capacity and control while avoiding any suspicion of strain.

(b) The output is as important as the intake. In the exercises described the breath should be allowed to flow out freely and the return of the ribs should be controlled and delayed according to the number of counts.

(c) It is possible to lay too much emphasis on capacity, which can lead to strained delivery and unnatural phrasing. Frequent intake is not a fault so long as it is related to sense and is unobtrusive. The speaking of a long passage on one breath is rarely called for in practice.

(d) A rigid chest should be guarded against: the aim throughout all breathing work is to keep the chest flexible. Rigidity and flexibility are reflected in vocal tone.

(*e*) In breathing, as in all voice work, there must be no hasty rushing into it: physical confidence and mental understanding should precede the action.

It is an advantage to begin breathing practice on the floor, preferably in the position described on page 19 under the heading SUPINE RELAXATION. In this position the ease of the body may be checked and a lengthened spread sensation encouraged. The back of the neck needs special attention to ensure the muscles "let go" and the root of the tongue should feel free. When air enters the lungs, it sometimes helps to imagine it enters through the eighth, ninth, tenth and eleventh back ribs. (Dr. Wilfred Barlow describes this as the "gill" position.) The slight fall of the sternum during expiration is more easily discerned in this position.

Up to the age of twelve years breathing exercises should not be formal. At about the age of twelve RIB SWING is taught. This improves the capacity of the breathing and imposes a simple control. The first five exercises establish this.

When not using the breath for speech the cycle of gentle effortless breathing is a slow intake, a slightly quicker output and then a pause. This cycle has to be altered when demands are going to be made on the breath. The first exercise equalizes the time of intake and the time of output.

1. Breathe in to a mental count of *In,2,3*.
Breathe *Out,2,3*.
(Repeat a few times).

The time of intake is gradually reduced and the time of output increased.

2. Breathe *In,2,3*.
Breathe *Out,2,3,4,5,6*.
Rest,*2,3*.

3. Breathe *In*, quickly but smoothly.
Breathe *Out,2,3,4,5,6*.

Further control of the breath is the next step.

4. Breathe *In,2,3,4,5,6*.
Breathe *Out,2,3* pause.
Breathe *Out,2,3*.

In these exercises care must be taken that there is no closure of the air passages. The pause must be made by maintaining a stationary position of the ribs and diaphragm.

5. Breathe *In*, quickly but smoothly.
Breathe *Out,2,3* pause.
Out,2,3, pause.
Out,2,3.

About the age of sixteen further control can be introduced if desired and RIB RESERVE BREATHING is one method used to achieve it. It should not supersede full chest breathing for meeting extra vocal demands but should be considered a valuable alternative. In rib reserve breathing a full chest breath is taken and then the ribs are held in an extended position. The diaphragm continues to move independently, contracting and going back to its original position, thus continuing the breathing process.

In this exercise the ribs are held out and the sensation of doing this should be recognized and carried into the following exercises. The exercise is to establish the feeling of holding the ribs in the extended position needed for rib reserve breathing.

Again, avoid a glottal closure during this exercise.

6. Breathe *In,2,3.*
   Pause,*2,3* (with the ribs held out).
   Breathe *Out,2,3.*
   Rest,*2,3.*
   (Repeat a few times).

Having learnt to hold the ribs out the next exercise is to learn the sensation of the diaphragm moving whilst the ribs remain in an extended position.

There should not be a false thrusting in and out of the epigastrium (the part of the body lying between the arch of the ribs).

7. Breathe *In,* taking a good chest breath.
   Keep the ribs held out and with only the diaphragm and abdominal muscles moving pant very gently through the open mouth being careful to ensure that the movement of the abdominal wall is correlated with the intake and output of the breath. At the end of the exercise Breathe *Out,* letting the ribs come in.

The movement of the diaphragm can now be extended so that the time of diaphragmatic intake and output is prolonged.

8. Breathe *In,* taking a good chest breath.
   Keep the ribs held out and continue breathing with the diaphragm only working. Take the breath in and out through the mouth.
   Breathe *Out,2,3.*
   Breathe *In,2,3.*
   Breathe *Out,2,3* etc.
   Finally breathe out and let the ribs come in.

Finally there should be a full rib reserve breathing exercise.

9. Breathe *In*, taking a good chest breath.

Hold the ribs out and with the diaphragm and abdominal muscles only working,

Breathe *Out*,*2*,*3*.

Renew the breath rapidly and gently through the mouth.

Repeat several times.

Finally breathe out, letting the ribs come in.

PART II: NOTE

SUMMARY

The note of the human voice is made by breath passing through the vibrating vocal folds (sometimes called the cords). If the laryngeal note were isolated it would be scarcely audible. It has to be passed through the resonators to become recognizable. The force of the breath attacking the vocal folds is directed from the diaphragm. The breath in this case is the excitor (or striking force).

The loudness of the sound depends upon the strength of the breath force and is called VOLUME. The more breath employed the louder the sound produced.

The PITCH is imposed by the larnyx and depends upon the length, mass and tenseness of the vocal folds. The longer the folds the lower the pitch; the greater the mass (thickness and weight) the lower the pitch; the tenser the folds the higher the pitch. The rule about length can be remembered if a man's larynx is compared with a woman's, and a woman's with a child's. The pitch rises in these three cases as the larynx becomes smaller. Mass can be explained by a length of elastic; the thicker it is, the lower the note when it is twanged. A piece of elastic can also demonstrate the change in pitch due to tenseness; if a certain length is pulled tight and twanged and the pitch noted, and then the same elastic is pulled tighter and twanged again, the second twang will be higher in pitch than the first because the elastic is tenser.

It is neither desirable nor advisable to think in a conscious way about the larynx and about pitch. The aim should be a happy and vital mental conception.

THE STRUCTURE OF THE LARYNX

The larynx is situated at the top of the trachea. It is suspended from the HYOID (tongue) BONE. Cartilages and muscles are arranged to form a long box to keep the breath passage open and protect the vocal folds.

HYOID BONE

THYROID

CRICOID

TRACHEA

DIAGRAM SHOWING THE POSITION OF THE LARYNX AND THE PROTECTING CARTILAGES

The trachea is kept open by incomplete rings of cartilage. The larynx rests on a complete ring at the top of the trachea called the CRICOID CARTILAGE. The larynx is mainly protected by the THYROID CARTILAGE which screens it in front but is open at the back. It can be seen in the neck as the "Adam's apple". The EPIGLOTTIS juts up over the opening of the larynx. The GLOTTIS is the space between the VOCAL FOLDS. These folds are the vibrator of the voice and stretch from the thyroid cartilage in front to the ARYTENOID CARTILAGES at the back. The arytenoids are triangular and are situated on the cricoid.

PHONATION

THE BREATH IS THE EXCITOR AND IT ATTACKS THE VIBRATOR (VIBRATING VOCAL FOLDS).

The nature of this vibration need not be investigated in detail. It is sufficient to know that the folds meet and part, causing a frequent stoppage in the outgoing breath stream. The effect of this repeated stoppage is that the breath becomes a vibrating column of air which passes into the resonators where it is given TONE (general quality). The vocal folds are approximated by the swivelling action of the arytenoid cartilages. When the pitch is mentally conceived the vocal folds vibrate at the frequency required to produce that note.

There are two aspects of the vocal folds which have to be considered. The first is their length; the size of the larynx plays a large part in giving height or depth to the voice. The second is the tension of the folds upon which variations of pitch depend. The tenser the folds the higher the pitch; the arytenoid cartilages tilt making the folds tighter.

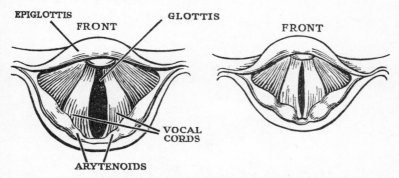

Left. DIAGRAM SHOWING THE GLOTTIS OPEN DURING BREATHING.
Right. DIAGRAM SHOWING THE GLOTTIS POSITIONED FOR SPEAKING.

Note. Vocal cords are now normally called vocal folds

THE NOTE AND VOCAL PRACTICE

Vocal practice should concentrate on a mental conception of the note. It is dangerous to be consciously aware of the working of the larynx.

The ear plays the controlling part in supplying the mental image needed to produce the note. The ear therefore must be trained and made sensitive to pitch; this training should be extended to reproducing the notes heard. A piano is essential for this work. As well as training the ear to the individual note, scales and melodies should be sung.

The attack of the breath on the vocal folds is a danger area in voice production. Without good breath control there is a tendency to manage the breath by closing the glottis and the result is a hard vocal attack. A slurred uncertain attack is equally to be avoided. The aim is an accurately attacked and vigorously sustained note.

Although in formation note precedes tone, in practice the resonators have to be exercised before vocalized breath is used. Specific exercises for note therefore have to follow those for tone.

PART III: TONE

SUMMARY

The original note made in the larynx by the interaction of breath and vocal folds is modified by the resonators. The pitch is imposed by the larynx and the resonators add general resonance which is TONE. The function of the resonators is to enhance the original note, giving it body and audibility. There are three main resonators, the pharynx (or neck), which is the first through which the vibrating column of breath passes; the mouth, lying at right angles to it and through which most of the breath passes out; the nose through which a small proportion of the breath passes out. Good tone depends upon a balance between these, each duly playing its part. This part cannot be undertaken by a resonator which is not in a good state of health. In addition to producing general quality the resonators contain the speech organs which produce particular quality, i.e. individual speech sounds.

THE STRUCTURE OF THE RESONATORS

THE PHARYNX

The important aspect of any resonator is that it is a hollow space. The pharynx and mouth share the ability to adjust their size and shape; the nose is constant in both size and shape.

The pharynx extends upwards from the larynx; it is bounded laterally by muscular walls and ends at the velum when this is raised. When this is lowered the pharynx continues into the

31

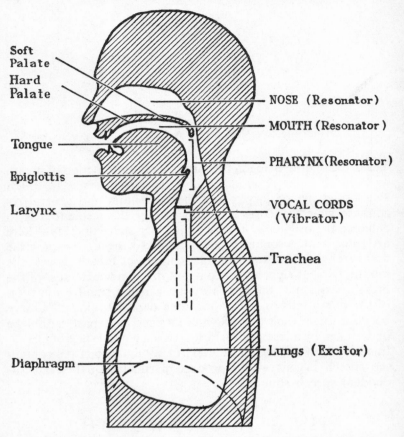

Soft Palate
Hard Palate
Tongue
Epiglottis
Larynx
Diaphragm

NOSE (Resonator)
MOUTH (Resonator)
PHARYNX (Resonator)
VOCAL CORDS (Vibrator)
Trachea
Lungs (Excitor)

DIAGRAMMATIC VIEW OF A VERTICAL SECTION THROUGH THE CHEST, PHARYNX, MOUTH AND NOSE

Note: The size of the nasal cavity is not really as large in proportion to the other cavities as it appears to be. Much of the space is filled with convoluted bone.

head cavity as the naso-pharynx. It can be sub-divided into:—
    the LARYNGOPHARYNX, the part just above the larynx;
    the OROPHARYNX, the part at the back of the mouth; and
    the NASOPHARYNX, the part opposite the nasal openings.
All these parts adjust in size and shape.

THE MOUTH

The mouth is bounded at the back by the oropharynx or by the velum when this is lowered. Its base is the tongue which is capable of flexible changes. The hard palate above is stable and does not change position. In the front the mouth is bounded by the lips which are also its ORIFICE (or opening) and can change size and shape considerably.

THE NOSE

The nose consists of a hollow space bounded by the internal bones of the head. It is divided in two by a long bone called the SEPTUM and is partially filled by scroll-like bones called TURBINATES. The bones within the head are partially hollowed to reduce weight. These hollowed bones are called SINUSES. They serve little purpose in voice production and can safely be disregarded. The amount of nasal resonance is controlled by the action of the velum.

RESONANCE

When a current of air is passed through a hollow space a RESONANT PITCH is heard.

If you take a large bottle with a small neck and blow through it a particular resonant pitch will be heard. Take another bottle of a different shape and size or with a different opening and a different resonant pitch will be heard.

Each hollow space has its own resonant pitch which depends on the size and shape of the hollow space and also upon the size and number of its openings. These openings are called ORIFICES.

The hollow space most actively concerned with vowel formation is the mouth. This will be considered first:—

When the jaw is dropped and the tongue is placed in various positions different vowel sounds are made. If these positions are breathed through each one will be found to have its own RESONANT PITCH in the same way that a current of air passing through any hollow space has its resonant pitch. Hollow spaces can be arranged in a sequence that enables a scale to be made of the resonant pitch.

The vowel shapes can be arranged so that the resonant pitches make a scale. Such an arrangement is known as a RESONATOR SCALE.

A series of identical bottles filled to differing heights can be hung in a sequence that results in a scale being heard when they are struck.

The sequence of the resonator scale derived from English vowel sounds begins with the back of the tongue raised close to the soft palate and the lips closely rounded. The back of the tongue lowers and the lips open progressively.

These in order are
    HOOT
    HOOK
    HOE
    HAWK
    HOCK
    HARD

The central vowels come next (these are vowels made by raising the centre of the tongue).

    HUT
    HEARD

Then the front of the tongue rises progressively through the next group until it is close to the hard palate and the last part of the sequence is formed.

    HAD
    HEAD
    HAY
    HID
    HEED

THE SEQUENCE OF THE RESONATOR SCALE is therefore: HOOT HOOK HOE HAWK HOCK HARD HUT HEARD HAD HEAD HAY HID HEED
(A useful mnemonic is WHO WOULD KNOW OUGHT OF ART MUST LEARN AND THEN TAKE HIS EASE. Each word to be pronounced with its full value as in isolation.)

Vowels are practised in this sequence using the whispered note only so that the resonant pitch is heard and checked. In considering TONE the resonant pitch of the neck has to be studied as well as that of the mouth.

Whisper through the sequence and hear the steady rise of the resonant pitch.

NECK (OR LOWER) RESONANCE

During the following explanation think of the mouth resonator and the neck resonator working separately and each supplying its own resonant pitch. In the following vowels HOOT HOOK HOE HAWK HARD the resonant pitches of the neck and mouth are separate but identical. After HARD the resonant pitch of the mouth continues to rise *but the Resonant Pitch of the Neck has a Descending Scale.* So as the positions pass from HARD to HEED (HARD HUT HEARD HAD HEAD HAY HID HEED) the resonant pitch of the mouth and the resonant pitch of the neck are different *and give two separate qualities to the tone.* This neck resonance is known as LOWER RESONANCE. Without sufficient lower resonance tone is thin and lacks body.

Neck resonance can be heard if the ears are completely covered when the resonator scale sequence is practised.

GOOD TONE DEPENDS ON BALANCED USE OF MOUTH, NECK AND NOSE RESONANCE

To understand the working of the human resonators in more detail two fundamental rules of resonance have to be grasped and applied:

1. The smaller the resonator the higher the pitch.
2. The smaller the orifice the lower the pitch.

The resonator scale begins with the vowel HOOT; the mouth orifice is small (close lip-rounding) therefore the resonant pitch is low. The lips become progressively more open as far as HARD and the resonant pitch rises as the orifice becomes larger. In the neck the resonant pitch is low for HOOT because the orifice (the opening between the back of the tongue and the soft palate) is small. From HOOT to HARD both the mouth and neck resonant pitch rises because both orifices become progressively larger. After HARD (actually after HUT: see the resonator scale) the resonant pitch of the mouth continues to rise because the front of the tongue rises steadily towards the hard palate making the resonator smaller and so raising the resonant pitch. In the neck meanwhile the orifice becomes steadily smaller as the front of the tongue rises towards the hard palate and so the resonant pitch falls. By the time HEED is reached the difference in the resonant pitch of the mouth and that of the neck exceeds an octave.

RESONATOR SCALE (AVERAGE WOMAN)

TONE AND VOCAL PRACTICE

In theory the sequence of BREATH, NOTE, TONE is a logical one. The excitor (the breath) is needed to attack the vibrator (the vocal cords) and the vibrating column of breath passes through the positioned resonators receiving resonance which is tone. In practice, however, the matter is not so simple. The resonators have to acquire good habits before the note is passed through them. Such habits depend partly on muscular skill and exercises for the speech organs (the movable parts of the resonators) have to precede exercises for positioning the resonators.

By the time tone is considered relaxation and good use of the body in exercises and in breathing should have helped in the attainment of a good physiological standard. A dynamic personal image infects the voice with lively, vital quality. A depressed, unimaginative outlook works to the detriment of tone. The aim is an accurate attack by well controlled breath on the vibrating vocal folds. The resultant tone has to be extended and given flexibility.

EXERCISES FOR THE SPEECH ORGANS

THE JAW

This must be free of tenseness and should open widely enough for the voice to pass out freely. It is the lower jaw that moves. It closes by muscular contraction; when this contraction ceases the jaw drops open. This easy effortless dropping down should be the image dominating all jaw work. Over-opening it can weaken tone.

These exercises must be watched in a mirror.

1. Smooth the jaw gently beginning from the hinged joints on either side and passing the fingers lightly down the cheeks to the chin. Do this slowly and induce a feeling of ease as the jaw falls open.

Running the fingers into the hair-line and massaging and loosening the skin over the temples can be a help. Care should be taken to see that the neck area is free from tension.

2. The second exercise is for agility. The lower jaw moves up and down slowly and easily. Rate is gradually increased until the movement is rapid. Tenseness must be avoided.

3. Chewing is the final exercise. This can be either real or imaginary. Both should be done with the lips open and the tongue working vigorously. Chewing a hard apple or a crisp carrot is very good for bringing blood into the gums and for making the jaw flexible.

THE LIPS

The labial muscle is circular and when it contracts the lips are made into a small circle. The size of this circle can be regulated. It is also possible to turn the upper lip up and the lower lip down. The lower lip offers little difficulty but exercises may be needed to make the

4. Look in a mirror and ease the lips. Let them lie softly together.

5. Turn the upper lip up; turn it back on itself. Help it with the finger if it refuses to move. Hold a pencil in the upper lip.

upper lip flexible. A stiff upper lip is an enemy to good voice and speech. If the sides of the lips are drawn-back the tone is thinned and articulation made more difficult.

6. Stroke the sides of the lips forward bringing about a pouting position.

7. Press the lips together flattening them.

8. Practise the various lip positions: neutral, open lip-rounding, and close lip-rounding. (See "Lip-shaping" under "Vowel Sounds", page 54).

THE TONGUE

The flexibility of the tongue has to be ensured by making it as economical and accurate in its movement as possible. Besides playing a part in the production of tone the tongue does much of the work of articulation.

9. Thrust the tongue out of the mouth into a sharp point making sure it does not go downhill but juts levelly from the mouth. It may help to hold a finger in front of the mouth and try to point the tongue to its top. When the tongue is withdrawn into the mouth its tip should contact the backs of the lower teeth. Repeat this exercise slowly, making sure the movement is accurate and gradually increase the speed of it. Accuracy is essential in tongue exercises. (Note: a few people possessing a short frenum may find these exercises cause soreness in which case they should not be done.)

10. Protrude the tongue into a point; raise the pointed tongue as high as possible and lower to as low a position as possible. Do not strain the tongue but do not be afraid of stretching it. Swing the tongue up and down several times.

11. Put out the tongue and point it. Then swing it to right and then to left as far as possible. Try to acquire the sensation of the swing and stretch of the tongue.

12. Put out the tongue and point it. Let the tongue spread out sideways. Then point it

hard again. Alternate these positions rhythmically.

13. Whirl the tongue round in a rhythmical movement.

14. Take an ice-cream cone or an ice lolly and holding it as far away from the mouth as the tongue can reach at a stretch, lick with the tongue in an upward, downward and circular movement. The ice cream is the reward but make sure the tongue works hard to gain it.

15. Close the lips but keep the jaw dropped. Move the tip of the tongue up to the teeth-ridge and down to the backs of the lower teeth. Increase the speed of the movement making sure it is accurate. Open the lips and repeat the exercise.

16. Keep the tip of the tongue contacting the backs of the lower teeth and raise the front to the HEED vowel position. Lower the tongue to the HARD position. Alternate these positions rapidly and accurately.

17. Keep the tip of the tongue contacting the backs of the lower teeth and raise the back of the tongue to a *k* position, then lower it to HARD. Alternate these positions rapidly.

18. Beginning with the tip of the tongue contacting the backs of the lower teeth raise the tip and tap the teeth-ridge with it. Do this as rapidly as possible.

The Soft Palate (Velum)

This is a difficult speech organ to exercise and it is difficult to watch. A

19. Keeping the mouth open breathe in through the nose

small torch shone into the mouth facilitates this.

and out through the mouth. Repeat this exercise watching the soft palate rise and fall.

20. Make a H*A*RD sound and then drop the soft palate so that the sound is nasalized and much of the breath passes out through the nose.

When these muscular exercises for the speech organs have been done awareness of the sensation of each organ should be increased.

EXERCISES TO INCREASE AWARENESS OF SENSATION IN THE SPEECH ORGANS

THE LIPS

1. Dampen the lips slightly. Put them together gently and hum quietly making the lips tingle. Then increase the power of the hum.

2. "Bumble" on the lips. Make a *b* sound in an easy bumbly way and repeat it. Aim at sounding like a bass drum.

3. Blow out through the lips making them roll. Do this up and down the scale.

4. Make the semi-vowel *w* and repeat it rapidly.

THE TONGUE

5. Hum on an *n* sound connecting the nasal sensation with that between the tip of the tongue and the teeth-ridge.

6. Repeat *d* rapidly but avoid slurring it.

7. Roll *r* on the tip of the tongue and sing it up and down the scale. It is a good test of breath control if the downwards scale can be sustained.

8. Make the semi-vowel beginning the word YET and repeat it rapidly.

THE SOFT PALATE

9. Hum on *ng* varying the pitch.

10. Repeat *g* rapidly, aiming at full voicing.

11. Roll an *r* sound between the uvula and the back of the tongue.

THE PURPOSE OF THE RESONATOR SCALE IN TONE EXERCISES

The previous exercises have prepared each speech organ SEPARATELY to play its part in the production of tone. The next step is to combine the speech organs to form a complete resonator. Each speech organ being flexible and controlled can maintain its position as part of the mouth resonator. This sustained position forms a pure vowel sound and the various positions of the resonator scale are identified by taking the name of the nearest vowel. The two diphthongs included in the resonator scale (HOE and HAY) have to be practised as pure vowels. This does NOT mean that they lose their diphthongal quality in actual speech where they should of course be practised as diphthongs.

As an introduction to the resonator scale a shortened version of it is used. This employs the five main sounds and arranges them thus:—

FIGURE OF EIGHT

	H*A*Y		H*A*WK	
H*EE*D		H*A*RD		H*OO*T
	H*A*Y		H*A*WK	

This arrangement begins with H*A*RD which is a convenient starting point because for this vowel the tongue is low in the mouth.

The principle is that the speech organs assume the position of the vowel and then the outgoing breath is passed steadily through it so that the Resonant Pitch is heard. (Resonant pitch is heard only when unvocalized breath is passed through the resonators. Resonant pitch should not be confused with vocal pitch).

The breath must pass out with good direction from the diaphragm; it should be a gentle, full outpouring, free from any rasping sound, with the resonant pitch audible only if the listener's ear is brought near the mouth. The ribs are kept extended and the sensation of controlling the breath from the diaphragm links up with the sensation of the breath passing out without restriction but through a steadily held physical position.

Certain points should be remembered in addition to those already described:—

(1) The vowel position must be accurate and free from tenseness.

(2) The jaw has to be comfortably but sufficiently open. The width depends upon the size of the individual mouth. For the opening measured between the front teeth $\frac{5}{8}$ of an inch is frequently sufficient; some people need far more. The open-jaw position must be kept as the speech organs move from position to position. The changes must not be made by jaw movement.

(3) There should be a renewal of breath between each vowel position. During the intake the new position is taken. A strong and clean attack on the new position is needed.

The figure-of-eight sequence moves from
HARD to HAY.

HAY is formed by raising the front of the tongue towards the hard palate. The next position is the close vowel

HEED. When this is made care must be taken not to over-tense the tongue and so produce a hard sound. Protruding the tongue is another fault.

After HEED the tongue lowers again and passes through HAY returning to HARD.

The back of the tongue then comes into play. It is essential to be aware of its rising action if the back vowels are to be accurately formed. The attitude that the lips only should be considered when the back vowels are practised is illogical and unsatisfactory to an intelligent student. If the rising action of the back of the tongue is understood due care can be taken to keep the muscular action free. In the second arm of the figure-of-eight the BACK of the tongue rises and the lips round. The halfway position is

H*AW*K.

To make this sound the back of the tongue is raised somewhat towards the soft palate and the lips are partially rounded. Finally, the back of the tongue rises to a close position and the lips move to a close lip-rounded position and the vowel produced is

H*OOT*.

The figure-of-eight returns to H*AW*K and back to H*A*RD.

When the sequence has been practised by whispering it, vocalized breath should be used.

The attack of the breath on the vowel position is of vital importance. A common fault during such practice is a hard vocal attack. This can be prevented by placing *h* before the vowel. This *h* can be retained mentally until good attack becomes a habit. Work on the resonator scale sequence not only ensures good tone as the resonators are used fully and in co-operation with good breath control but also enables the vowel positions to be learned and practised. Accuracy should be the aim of vowel positioning. The change from one position to another should be done with as much economy as possible.

When the resonant pitch is correct, well attacked and sustained, the next stage is to pass vocalized breath through the positioned resonators and so make TONE. The vibrating column of air will receive one quality as it passes through the neck and another as it passes through the mouth. When the vowel position has a different resonant pitch in the mouth from the neck (H*A*RD to HEED) the double quality is distinguishable. It is particularly easy to hear in HEED.

The neck gives warm deep quality to tone and this is LOWER

RESONANCE; it gives the voice "body". It is easily heard in high voices and gives the backing to the tone which prevents a high voice being thin and reedy.

TONE EXERCISES

(1) Work on the figure-of-eight on the principle already described in detail above.

(2) Extension of these exercises to the full resonator-scale sequence.

These achieve well balanced tone resulting from a well directed breath force passing through correctly positioned resonators.

(3) Humming on *m*. This begins quietly humming into cupped hands. The mask of the face should "come alive". An illusion of humming well outside the mouth gives the breath strength and direction.

(4) Humming on *n* concentrating on a buzzing through the nose.

(5) Humming on *ng*. The naso-pharynx responds to this and the inside of the head has a vibrating sensation.

(6) The resonator scale sequence can be combined with the nasal sounds in the following ways:

      (*a*) in initial positions,

      (*b*) in final positions,

      (*c*) initially and finally,

      (*d*) in an inter-vowel position (or "medial" position).

(7) Any consonants can be combined with the vowel sequence for practice. Particularly valuable ones for tone are:

      b d g v *TH*EN z MEASURE w y

(8) Sung scales are a vital part of voice training and must be done to a piano accompaniment. Such scales are valuable in training pitch; they extend the range and flexibility of the speaking voice.

At this point exercises for tone merge into vocal application and further ones are given on page 80.

COMMON FAULTS OF TONE

(1) It is possible to have too much lower resonance. The effect of this is a "booming" undertone. It is a sign of inexpert voice training.

(2) Another common fault is for the voice to be over-resonant. This again is a fault due to poor training. The effect is of "noise". Clarity is marred and flexibility impeded as well as the voice being difficult to listen to.

(3) Hard vocal attack has already been described and is often a sign of general tenseness which makes the tone thin and hard.

(4) Insufficient breath can harden tone because instead of the diaphragm controlling adequate outgoing breath, the upper chest is tensed to drive out the breath with sufficient force to make phonation possible.

(5) Weak faltering tone is another fault due to inadequate breath.

(6) When the balance of resonance is considered the nose as well as the mouth and neck plays a vital part. This part is more obvious when the nose is not in a healthy state.

In English, except for the nasal sounds *m*, *n* and *ng*, the soft palate is raised towards the back wall of the pharynx and this considerably reduces the amount of breath passing out through the nose. When it is raised towards the wall of the pharynx there is space for some breath to pass out through the nose. This gives the tone nasal resonance.

There are many faults covered by the term "nasal tone". If the soft palate is insufficiently raised, too much breath passes out through the nose and the tone is excessively nasal. This is a HYPER-RHINO condition (*hyper*, over-much; *rhino*, nose). When the nasal passage is blocked and no breath passes out through it the tone again sounds nasal and this is a HYPO-RHINO condition (*hypo*, under; *rhino*, nose). The terms are unimportant except for supplying a convenient label for these forms of nasality. There is a third common cause of nasality and its effect sounds very like the others; this is muscular tenseness. A fourth form of nasality is caused by slight irregularities of the bones of the nasal cavities.

PART IV: WORD

SUMMARY

The general function of the resonators is to produce tone; their particular function is to produce speech sounds. This is done by particular parts of the oral resonator known as speech organs. Vowels are made by vocalized breath passing freely through the mouth and the speech organs positioning to impose a particular shape on it. Consonants are made by the speech organs positioning to impede the passage of the outgoing breath. Vowels and consonants group together to form words. Sounds cannot be made without air being set in motion. We speak of the pulmonic egressive air-stream (pulmonic, from the lungs; egressive, outgoing; air-stream, note that it is moving).

THE SPEECH ORGANS

VIEW OF THE INSIDE OF THE MOUTH SEEN FROM THE FRONT
U, Uvula; *T*, Tonsils (if present); *P*, Pharynx.

Working from the lips inwards the speech organs are:

46

LIPS

These are the free edges of the mouth. They are opened by dropping the jaw. There is a muscle running round the lips and by its contraction the lips move and make the lip positions required for some speech sounds.

Look in a mirror and study each speech organ observing its various movements. Connect the speech sounds with parts of the mouth.

JAW

The lower jaw bone is attached to the facial bones by hinge joints. It is in an open position for most speech sounds.

Observe the jaw positions when the following sounds are made
s   f   HARD

TEETH

These are attached in curved rows to the upper and lower jaws. The upper front teeth, the incisors and canines, overlap the lower jaw teeth.

Observe your own tooth formation and the way in which breath is affected by them during the formation of *f v f*ast *v*ast *th th*in *th*en.

TEETH-RIDGE (OR ALVEOLAR RIDGE)

This is the ridge between the upper teeth and the curving hard palate.

Several consonants are articulated against this ridge. Feel it with the tongue-tip and practise *t d n r l.*

HARD PALATE

This forms the roof of the mouth and separates it from the nasal cavity. Its foundation is a horizontal bone arch.

Study this arch in the mirror and trace it with the tongue-tip.

SOFT PALATE

The hard palate forms two-thirds of the whole palate. The back third is the soft palate. It continues from the hard palate and is arched. Its back edge is free and from the middle of it there is a projection called the UVULA. The tonsils are embedded in it, one on each side of the uvula. The back part of the

Drop the jaw and breathe in through the mouth and out through the nose keeping the mouth open. The movement of the soft palate will be seen.

soft palate can move freely. Another term for the soft palate is the VELUM.

TONGUE

This lies on the floor of the mouth and turns at a right angle to form part of the front wall of the pharynx. The mouth part of the tongue is free and the tip and sides touch the teeth. The tongue is largely formed of muscle and so is very mobile. Underneath the tongue attaching it to the floor of the mouth is a ligament called the FRENUM.

Parts of the tongue (these do not correspond to any anatomical features but are convenient divisions for the classification of speech sounds):

TIP: the point of the tongue.

BLADE: the part underneath the upper teeth-ridge when the tongue is at rest.

FRONT: this lies under the hard palate.

CENTRE: this lies partly under the hard palate and partly under the soft.

BACK: the part underneath the soft palate.

These are the parts of the tongue concerned with speech. They lie in the mouth and make up the part that can be seen when the mouth is opened.

ROOT: this lies in the throat.

Study your own tongue and identify the parts.

VOCAL FOLDS (OR VOCAL CORDS).

These are a pair of free edges running from front to back across the larynx. The space between them is the glottis.

Besides vibrating and so vocalizing the breath the vocal folds are also a speech organ. The plosive sound made by them in the same way as the lips make *p* is not a recognized sound in English although it is used extensively. The fricative consonant *h* is the friction produced as breath passes through the narrowed glottis.

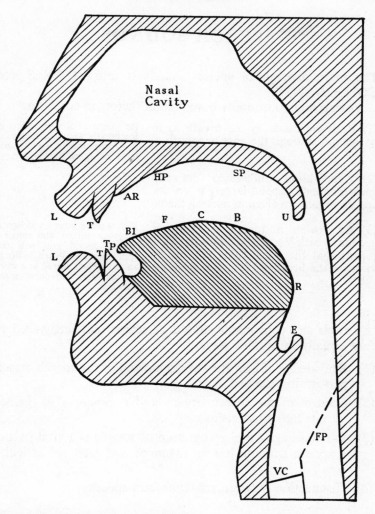

DIAGRAMMATIC VIEW OF A SECTION THROUGH NOSE, MOUTH AND NECK
SHOWING THE PARTS OF THE MOUTH USED IN DESCRIBING SPEECH SOUNDS

L, Lips; *T*, Teeth; *AR*, Alveolar Ridge; *HP*, Hard Palate; *SP*, Soft
Palate; *U*, Uvula; *VC*, Vocal folds or cords; *FP*, Food Passage
Tongue: *Tp*, Tip; *Bl*, Blade; *F*, Front; *C*, Centre; *B*, Back.
The Soft Palate is shown in the lowered position.

SPEECH SOUNDS

The main division of speech sounds is into VOWELS and CONSONANTS.

Vowels and consonants have certain factors in common:

(1) Both are made by the breath as it passes out through the nose or mouth.

Be aware of the sensation of the breath. Learn to recognize the formation of vowels and consonants by "feeling" them.

(2) Individual differences between speech sounds depend largely upon the speech organs involved in making them.

(3) All vowels and some consonants are made with VOCALIZED BREATH. This means that the vocal folds vibrate or vocalize the breath as it passes through them.

If you place your hand lightly on your throat and make a voiced sound you will feel this vibration. When in doubt as to whether sound in a word is voiced or unvoiced make this test.

Vowels and consonants should be learnt and recognized in four equally important ways:

(1) Knowledge of how they are made and of the speech organs performing the task.

(2) Control of the speech organs and muscular skill (gained by intelligent exercising).

(3) Ear training. Aural recognition of sounds is a vital part of a speech training lesson. (Manner and place of articulation.)

(4) Connection between sensation and speech.

VOWELS

A Vowel is made by vocalized breath passing through the mouth. The individual quality of each Vowel is imposed by the positioning of the speech organs.

Vowels divide into
   (*a*) PURE VOWELS and
   (*b*) DIPHTHONGS

PURE VOWELS

During the formation of these vowels the speech organs are held in one position.

The tongue is mainly responsible for the formation of vowels. The principal factor in determining the nature of a vowel is the part of the tongue which is raised and the height to which it is raised.

For purposes of classification of vowels the tongue is divided into

FRONT

CENTRE

BACK

If the tongue is raised near to the roof of the mouth it is a CLOSE position. If the tongue is low it is an OPEN position.

Two points should be remembered when vowels are practised:
1. The jaw should be open and easy.
2. The tip of the tongue should contact the backs of the lower front teeth.

Always practise vowel shaping with a mirror. Look in it and check the positions.

A good vowel sound depends upon:
1. An accurate positioning of the speech organs.
2. A steadily held position.
3. A steady breath stream.

Put a clean spoon on the front of your tongue and say the vowels
   H*A*D and H*EE*D.
The first is low and the second high.

FRONT-OF-TONGUE
   VOWELS
Drop the jaw and make sure the tip of the tongue is contacting the backs of the lower teeth.

The FRONT of the tongue is the part lying under the hard palate. Watch this part of the tongue and make the lowest most open English front vowel
HAD.
Pass on to the next one which is a little higher in position
HEAD.
Then say
HID.
and finally
HEED.

HID and HEED will be seen to be close vowels with the tongue raised near the palate. For HEED it is very close.

From this an arrangement of these vowels can be made:

FRONT OF TONGUE

HEED (CLOSE) Tongue high in the mouth.

HID

HEAD

HAD (OPEN) Tongue low in mouth.

BACK-OF-TONGUE VOWELS

These are difficult to observe because they have a lip articulation as well as the tongue position. When these vowels are practised during speech lessons the accuracy of the sound is achieved by the ear and attention is concentrated on the lip position. A clean finger placed on the back of the tongue will enable the rise of the back of the tongue to be felt. The BACK of the tongue is the part underneath the soft palate.

Beginning with the back of the tongue low in the mouth make the vowel
HARD.
This vowel and the vowel

HUT are often regarded as back of tongue vowels but in fact they are made with the centre of the tongue today. They are shown in a centralized position on the chart.

Follow with the vowels HOCK and HAWK. For this sequence the back of the tongue rises slightly. HUT is about on a height with HAWK and its central position has already been considered.

The last two back vowels are close and so the tongue is high when they are made. They are HOOK and HOOT.

The back-of-tongue vowels can be arranged thus:

BACK OF TONGUE

	HOOT	TONGUE HIGH IN MOUTH (CLOSE VOWEL POSITION)
	HOOK	
	HAWK	TONGUE LOW IN MOUTH (OPEN VOWEL POSITION)
HUT	HOCK	
HARD		

From these positions it will be seen that each vowel has a separate position and that vowels cannot be coupled in pairs as short and long versions of one sound. For example HEED is a close front vowel sound and is long. It is not a lengthened version of HID, which has a lower front tongue position. The difference in tongue position can be seen and felt.

Practise the front vowels from HAD to HEED and watch the front of the tongue rising (keep the tip low). Practise the back vowels from HARD to HOOT, remembering that most of them also have a lip-shaping.

Front, centre and back vowels can be put together to form a plan of pure vowels.

Front of Tongue	Centre of Tongue	Back of Tongue	
HEED		HOOT	TONGUE HIGH IN MOUTH
HID		HOOK	(CLOSE VOWEL POSITION)
HEAD	HEARD		
	ABOUT		
		HAWK	
HAD	HUT	HOCK	TONGUE LOW IN MOUTH
	HARD		(OPEN VOWEL POSITION)

LIP-SHAPING

The lip-shaping which several back vowels have is vital to their formation. It is possible to make a clearly recognizable vowel sound without lip-rounding by compensating for the absence of this by means of a different tongue position. The lip and tongue positions as described are however recommended in order to achieve the best result.

NEUTRAL LIP POSITION

Most vowels have a neutral lip position. This illustration shows a width of jaw opening such as would be used in speaking in a loud voice. Vowels should be practised with this wide jaw opening.

This illustration shows the lips in a neutral position with a medium jaw opening likely to be used in quiet speech.

OPEN LIP ROUNDING

One vowel has open lip rounding. It is HOCK. The jaw position shown is an open one.

MEDIUM LIP ROUNDING

Two vowels have medium lip rounding. These are H*OO*K and H*A*WK. The illustration shows an open jaw position.

CLOSE LIP ROUNDING

This shows the close lip rounding used for the vowel H*OO*T.

When these vowels are either the starting point or the finishing point of a diphthong the appropriate degree of lip rounding is used.

Vowel Length

The length of a vowel (the length of time it is sustained) depends on its position in the word. Luckily if English is one's mother-tongue this does not have to be consciously learnt and applied.

In the following list the length shortens:

H*E* (Very long in this open position.)
H*EE*D (The vowel shortens when followed by a consonant.)
H*EA*T (A consonant without voice shortens it yet more.)
H*EA*TING (The vowel is shorter still when another syllable follows.)

Knowledge of this form of vowel length is only important to avoid undue lengthening of vowels in an effort to clarify or improve speech. If vowels are given undue length the balance of enunciation is upset and the speech does not sound natural. However in spite of these slight variations some vowels are intrinsically long and some are intrinsically short.

LONG VOWELS

These include all diphthongs and the following pure vowels:

H*EE*D

HE*AR*D
H*AR*D
H*A*WK
H*OO*T

You may be aware of a slight diphthongal glide when you say H*EE*D and H*OO*T. They are pure vowels but are only relatively so. The glide is not long enough for them to be classed as diphthongs.

SHORT VOWELS

H*I*D
HE*A*D
H*A*D
*A*BOUT
H*U*T
H*O*CK
H*OO*K

THE EFFECT OF EMPHASIS AND WORD STRESS ON VOWEL LENGTH

The relationships of vowel length already described apply when vowels are compared in identical circumstances. Emphasis placed on a word will tend to lengthen the vowel in that word (or stressed syllable of that word) even if this is normally a short vowel.

Many people would considerably lengthen the short vowel in the word "bad" when stressing the word in a phrase such as "It's thoroughly b*a*d".

Conversely a normally long vowel in an unstressed syllable may be quite short.

Compare the length of the vowel in the first syllable of "August" (month of the year) in which this vowel receives word stress with the length of this vowel in the word "august" (adjective) in which the word stress is on the second syllable.

DIPHTHONGS

The speech organs making a diphthong move throughout its formation. The result of this movement is a glide. A diphthong is defined as

A continuous glide from one vowel position towards a second.

There are nine English diphthongs. All are falling diphthongs: this means that the weight comes at the beginning of the glide. The nine divide into

FOUR CENTRING DIPHTHONGS and

FIVE CLOSING DIPHTHONGS.

CENTRING DIPHTHONGS

To make these glides the speech organs begin in a front or back vowel position and glide towards the central vowel *A*BOUT.

H*ERE* begins at H*I*D and glides towards *A*BOUT.

H*ARE* begins at HE*A*D (said with a low tongue position) and glides towards *A*BOUT.

HO*AR* begins at HA*W*K and glides towards *A*BOUT.

T*OUR* begins at HO*O*K and glides towards *A*BOUT.

CLOSING DIPHTHONGS

To make these glides the tongue rises in the mouth. It moves from one vowel position to a second which is closer (or nearer) to the roof of the mouth.

H*AY* begins at HE*A*D and glides towards H*I*D.

(This is a short glide made by the front of the tongue.)

H*IGH* begins at an open (low) front tongue position and glides towards H*I*D.

(This is a long glide made by the front of the tongue.)

H*OW* begins at an open (low) central tongue position and glides towards HO*O*K.

(This is a long glide passing from an open central position towards a fairly close back one.)

H*OY* begins at HA*W*K said with a low tongue position and glides towards H*I*D.

(This is a long glide from a fairly open back position through the centre tongue towards a front fairly close position.)

H*OE* begins at a fairly close (high) central position and glides towards HO*O*K.

(This is a short glide made from the centre of the tongue towards a closer back position.)

In H*O*AR, T*O*UR, H*O*W, H*O*Y and H*O*E vowels are involved which have lip rounding and the appropriate degree should be used when making the diphthong.

Remember all vowels are practised with a low tip of tongue position. Maintain this position when practising diphthongs.

Avoid making two sounds when a diphthong is spoken. The aim should be a gradual and continuous movement of the speech organs concerned and the result a glide.

TRIPHTHONGS

Words in which so-called triphthongs are said to occur are either two syllables or diphthongs according to the way in which they are pronounced. The student must be content with this dogmatic statement, as only a phonetician can appreciate the explanation.

From the practical point of view triphthongs can be disregarded.

CONSONANTS

Whereas a vowel must have a free passage through the mouth a consonant is made by the outgoing breath being impeded in some way. These ways are various and the nature of several of them can be guessed from their names.

A PLOSIVE is connected with an explosion.

A NASAL obviously must be a sound made through the nose.

LATERAL (or sideways) can refer to only one sound in English (*l*).

A FRICATIVE must be sound with friction in it.

Some consonants are made with unvocalized breath and some with vocalized breath. All consonants are made with the velum raised, except the nasals (in the formation of which the breath goes out through the nose).

Consonants made with vocalized breath are known as
VOICED.

Consonants not made with vocalized breath are known as
UNVOICED.

Voiced consonants are made with weaker breath pressure
than their unvoiced counterparts.

Here is a list of ways in which the breath escapes and the
resultant sounds:

PLOSIVE CONSONANTS

These are made by a total blockage
of the air passage through the mouth by
contact between two speech organs.
Breath pressure increases behind the
contact (this is called the HOLD or
STOP) and an explosion is heard when
the organs part.

p	b
t	d
k	g

AFFRICATE CONSONANTS

These begin in the same way as
plosives with the contact and hold of
two speech organs. Instead of a quick
clean release there is a gradual release
and friction is heard as the organs part.
An affricate is one sound.

       *ch*in *g*in
or *ch*eer *j*eer

NASAL CONSONANTS

In making these the mouth passage is
completely blocked by the contact of
two speech organs and the soft palate
lowers so that all the air passes out
through the nose resulting in a nasal
sound.

    m
    n
  si*ng*

LATERAL CONSONANTS

When the middle of the outgoing air
passage is blocked (by raising the tongue

  *l*ane
  fu*ll*

to contact the teeth-ridge but keeping the sides lowered) the breath escapes sideways or laterally.

ROLLED AND FLAPPED CONSONANTS

A flapped consonant is made by the contact and release of two speech organs (there is no hold- and build-up of air pressure as with a plosive). A rolled consonant is two or more flaps repeated. It is similar to a drum-roll. In Received Pronunciation (consciously acquired accurate speech) the tongue taps once only at the back of the teeth-ridge to make flapped *r*.

spirit

FRICATIVE CONSONANTS

Friction is heard when two speech organs are very close together so narrowing the passage of the outgoing breath.

*th*in   *th*en
f   *v*
s   *z*
*s*ure   mea*s*ure
h
  r

SEMI-VOWELS

These begin in the position of very close vowels and the sound consists of a rapid movement (or glide) towards another vowel. They are classed as consonants because they function as such.

w
y

THE ORGANS MAKING CONSONANTS

When the nature of consonant sounds has been grasped the question of which organs make them has to be considered.

LABIAL to do with the lips.

BI-LABIAL to do with both lips.

DENTAL to do with the teeth.

ALVEOLAR to do with the teeth-ridge (alveolar ridge).

LINGUAL to do with the tongue.

VELAR to do with the soft palate (velum).

PALATAL to do with the hard palate.

GLOTTAL to do with the vocal cords (the glottis is the space between the vocal cords).

A simple chart can be made, as shown below.

CONSONANT CHART

	Bi-labial	Labio-dental	Dental	Alveolar	Palato-alveolar	Palatal	Velar	Glottal
LOSIVES	p b			t d			k g	
FFRICATES					*ch*in *g*in			
ASALS	m			n			si*ng*	
ATERALS				*l*ane fu*ll*				
RICATIVES		f v	*th*in *th*en	s z	*s*ure mea*s*ure			h
LAPPED				r				
MI-VOWELS	w					*y*et		

DETAILS OF THE CONSONANTS

TO MAKE:

p the lips come together; breath pressure increases whilst they are together; when they part an explosive sound is heard.

Remember it takes time to learn to know and recognize sounds.

b the process is the same as for *p* but the breath force is weaker and the sound is voiced, as the vibrating vocal cords vocalize the outgoing breath.

t the tip of the tongue rises and touches the teeth-ridge; breath pressure increases during this contact; an explosive sound is heard when the tip of the tongue is quickly removed.

The teeth-ridge can be felt. It is the clearly marked rather bumpy ridge behind the upper teeth.

d the process is the same as for *t* but the breath force is weaker and it is voiced.

In whispered speech it is the weaker breath pressure of voiced consonants that enables them to be distinguished from their voiceless counterparts.

k is made by the back of the tongue rising to touch the soft palate; breath pressure increases during the contact; when the tongue lowers an explosive sound is heard.

The soft palate is the soft movable part of the roof of the mouth behind the hard palate. It can be felt with the tongue.

g the process is the same as for k but the breath pressure is weaker and it is voiced.

chin is made by the tip of the tongue rising and contacting the teeth-ridge; the front of the tongue rises towards the hard palate; the breath pressure increases during the tip-of-tongue contact; instead of a quick clean release being made the tip of the tongue comes away slowly and friction is heard between the front of the tongue and the hard palate.

This slow release of a plosive resulting in the addition of a fricative consonant is known as AFFRICATION.

gin is made in the same way as chin except that it is voiced.

m is made by the lips coming together so that there is no way out for the breath except over the top of the soft palate, which is lowered to let the breath pass out through the nose. It is a voiced sound.

If you make an m and then take all the voice out of it you will feel a strong current of air passing down the nose.

n is made in the same way as m except that the mouth opening is closed by the tip of the tongue rising and contacting the teeth-ridge.

sing is made in the same way as m except that the mouth opening is cut off by the contact of the back of the tongue which is raised to the soft palate which is lowered.

lane is made by the tip of the tongue rising and contacting the teeth-ridge; the sides of the tongue are in a lowered position; the breath escapes from the mouth by going round the middle obstruction made by the tongue. Consequently the breath

This sideways escape can be plainly felt if the voice is taken out of the sound. l before a vowel is a CLEAR l.

escapes sideways or laterally. It is a voiced sound. In clear *l* the front of the tongue is raised towards the hard palate giving a "vowel resonance" similar to H*I*D.

DIAGRAM SHOWING THE POSITION OF THE TONGUE AND SOFT PALATE DURING THE FORMATION OF "SI*NG*"

Sagittal section through the median line of the tongue.

fu*ll* is made in the same way as clear *l* except that the front of the tongue is low and the back is raised towards the soft palate giving a quality reminiscent of the vowel in H*OO*K.

This is DARK *l* and is used in a final position and before a consonant.

*th*in is made by the tip of the tongue being placed so near the upper teeth that only a very narrow air passage is left; friction is heard as the breath passes through this.

*th*en is made in the same way as *th*in, except that it is voiced.

f is the audible friction heard when the upper teeth and the lower lip touch and breath is forced out between them.

It is the inside of the lower lip that makes the sound. Don't "bite" the lip.

v is made in the same way as *f* except that it is voiced.

s is made by the breath being forced through a narrow groove made by the sides of the tongue touching the roof of the mouth leaving a channel down the middle.

The friction is made in the narrow gap between the blade of the tongue and the teeth-ridge. Secondary articulation may occur between the tip of the tongue and the teeth.

z is made in the same way as *s* but it is voiced.

*s*ure is made by sending the breath through a groove made by the tongue against the hard palate and teeth-ridge; the groove is not so narrow as it is in *s* but friction occurs over a longer distance. The lips are usually but not necessarily protruded.

The particularly piercing quality of this sound enables it to be used to penetrate a babble of conversation and secure attention.

mea*s*ure is made in the same way as *s*ure but is voiced.

h is made when the vocal cords are sufficiently approximated to produce audible friction as breath passes between them.

h can be demonstrated by taking the voice out of any vowel.

*r*un is made by raising the tip of the tongue very close to the back of the teeth-ridge. Friction is heard as the breath passes out. It is a voiced sound.

Fricative *r* is used in Received Pronunciation in all positions except that the flapped variety is used by some speakers between vowels.
Examples of the use of flapped *r* are:

pe*r*iod is flapped or "one-tap" *r* and is made by the tip of the tongue tapping once against the back of the teeth-ridge. It is a voiced sound.

(*a*) within a word; for example, Mary, period, hurry.
(*b*) as LINKING *r* in phrases such as "far away", "her age". Many people find it easier to sound the *r* at the end of a word when the next word begins with a vowel.
When flapped *r* is used it gives the speech extra clarity.

w has its primary articulation made by the lips. A raising of the back of the tongue also takes place as a secondary articulation. Both lips and tongue immediately glide towards the vowel following and it is this glide which makes the sound.

yet is made by the front of the tongue rising very close to the hard palate and gliding immediately towards another vowel.

Semi-vowels are very near to being vowels but it is preferable to regard them as consonants because (a) they cannot be sustained and (b) they behave as consonants in that the pre-consonantal form of the indefinite article is used before words beginning with them. For example "a yard" not "an yard" and "a wood" and not "an wood".

VOWELS AND CONSONANTS IN CONNECTED SPEECH

So far each sound has been considered as a separate entity. When sounds are linked together to form syllables what is heard is not a series of separate sounds but a series of sounds merging into each other. Between two voiced sounds vocalization continues and as the speech organs move into position to make the second sound a slight speech glide is heard.

In connected speech sounds are rarely given their full value. Slight changes come about because the sound is easier to say if it is slightly modified.

PHONEMIC VARIANTS

Sounds in a language have slight changes caused by neighbouring sounds. PHONEME is another term for speech sounds as used in this book. Phonemic variants are modifications made to a sound by the influence of its neighbouring sounds. The slight variations in the sounds keep the word easily recognizable and in no way change the meaning.

As an example some of the phonemic variants of k are considered here. Speak the word KEEN and notice the lip position of k (neutral). Now say the same sounds with a w between k and H*EE*D saying the word QUEEN and you will find that the strong lip rounding of w makes k also lip rounded.

Speak KEEN noticing the place of articulation between the back of the tongue and the soft palate. Now speak COON and you will find the place of articulation has moved back considerably. This is through the influence of the back tongue position of the vowel following the k in COON.

Another variant is the amount of aspiration which follows the plosion of k.

The aspiration is generally less at this end of a syllable than at the beginning: compare KATE and TAKE.

Frequently when one plosive is followed by another the first of the pair is not exploded. In the phrase LOOK KATE the contact and hold of the first k are made, then there is a fresh impetus or push o energy and the hold and release of the second k (KATE) is made. This INCOMPLETE PLOSION of a plosive consonant is very common and is not confined to identical consonants. Examples are:

A*C*T
BI*G* POLES
BRIGH*T* DAY
BRIGH*T* STAR

Another phonemic variant of k is when it is exploded sideways or laterally. This is illustrated in the word BUCKLE. The k is exploded sideways through the influence of the lateral l sound following.

The importance of phonemic variants is not in having detailed knowledge of them but in realizing their existence and in keeping the spoken language natural by not speaking each sound as it is made when pronounced in isolation. Balanced accurate enunciation depends upon the use of the correct phonemic variant. If one's mother tongue is English phonemic variants do not have to be learnt: they are part of the natural flow of the language. The effect of using the wrong phonemic variant is either one of regional accent or of over-care and affectation.

LATERAL PLOSION

When a plosive consonant is followed by an *l* sound it is released through the *l* position sideways or laterally.

The lateral plosion can be heard when the sounds are at the beginning of a syllable. This lateral quality is an essential part of the formation of *l* and it influences the preceding plosive.

Say the words PLEASE, CLOVER and experience the sideways explosion of the *p* and *k*.

The lateral plosion is often found more difficult when it forms the second syllable of a word such as BOT*TL*E, BUC*KL*E, PEO*PL*E.

Practise the words BOTTLE, BUCKLE, PEOPLE, and avoid making a vowel between the plosive and the *l*.

Another frequent use of phonemic variants is in

NASAL PLOSION

When a plosive consonant is released through the nose instead of the mouth it is said to have a nasal plosion. This happens in words in which the plosive is followed by a nasal consonant made in the same articulatory position.

t is exploded through *n* in words such as BUTTON, WRITTEN. The tongue. remains on the teeth-ridge and the breath escapes through the nose when the soft palate lowers to make the *n* sound.

Say the word BUTTON. No vowel sound should be made between the *t* and *n*. Other examples are HIDDEN and GARDEN.

Sometimes in connected speech neighbouring sounds cause the replacement of sounds by new ones not phonemic variants of the original. This is known as

ASSIMILATION

This is the process of replacing a sound in a word by another sound because of the strong influence of a third neighbouring sound near it in the word or sentence. An example will make this clear.

Speak the phrase IN TEN MINUTES. The *n* of TEN often becomes an *m*: TEM MINUTES. *n* and *m* have in common the fact that they are nasals but the bilabial influence of the *m* of MINUTES has influenced the alveolar *n* and made it also bilabial.
Other examples are:
JOHN BROOK might become JOHM BROOK; CAN BE— CAM BE; HAND CARVED —HANG CARVED.

Too much assimilation in speech gives the effect of careless enunciation and is to be avoided. A degree of it has to be accepted especially when speech is informal. Assimilation is most likely to occur in more rapid styles of speech.

Not only do sounds vary in connected speech. The position of a sound in a word or sentence can lead to its omission. This process is called

ELISION

The question of whether a sound is elided depends on its place in a word and the importance of the word in a sentence. A stressed word is less likely to have elided sounds.

A sound frequently elided is *h*.

In a sentence such as THEY MAY HAVE BEEN the *h* of HAVE is likely to be elided.

Sounds in parts of verbs are apt to be elided.

IT IS LIKELY becomes IT'S LIKELY.

IT HAS NOT HAPPENED
becomes
IT HASN'T HAPPENED.

The connecting word AND is an example.

TOWN AND COUNTRY has the *d* of AND elided. Take a paragraph. Read it aloud but do not leave out any sound which you would normally put into the word when pronounced by itself. Then take the same paragraph and read it as you would speak it naturally and mark the sounds you have elided.

Another interesting feature of connected speech is

GRADATION

It is possible to have more than one pronunciation of a word occurring in spoken English. Some words have a STRONG form which is heard when the word is stressed and a WEAK form which is heard when the word is in an unimportant position in a sentence. This use of strong and weak forms of the same word is GRADATION.

Gradation gives the natural flow to language. The words are given their weak form because it is easier to say them that way.

Examples of this are seen in the phrase THE BOY in which the vowel in THE is *A*BOUT and not H*EE*D.

This happens before words which begin with consonants. If the following word begins with a vowel this is pronounced either with a shortened version of H*EE*D or with H*I*D.

There are different styles of speech varying from the COLLOQUIAL to the FORMAL. As one would expect the latter includes few weak forms but the former has quite a number.

Speak the sentence THERE ARE TWO OF THEM and observe the gradation.

THE WORD AND CONNECTED SPEECH

Spoken language relies on PAUSE, STRESS and INTONATION to give it meaning and significance.

PAUSE

In speech a pause is a cessation of sound. Pauses are used in all connected speech to mark the sense; they are oral punctuation. The sense can often be further clarified and enhanced by pauses which are not strictly in line with the grammatical construction of the sentence. A word can be given importance by pausing before and after it, thus isolating it and bringing it into prominence. A pause builds up the suspense and it is useful when climax is being reached or when a strong emotional situation is being interpreted. Pauses should be carefully timed. Overlong pauses can break the sense and the feeling during performance. This is particularly so when an audience is present and whose reaction has to be considered as well as the meaning of the words being spoken.

In poetry pause has a special part to play in giving the pattern to verse-form. The end-of-line pause can be a final one with a full stop marking the end of the sentence, or a colon, semicolon or comma marking the end of a phrase. When this happens in a poem it is known as an end-stopped line.

Good poets frequently run their sense from one line into the next without a final pause at the line ending. This run-on line is sometimes called an enjambed line. When this occurs one must convey the effect of the sense spilling over into the next line. A pause is made to mark the ending of the first line. The last word of the line is suspended by intonation and duration in order to point forward to a continuation of the sense into the second line; and then a fresh impetus is given to the first word of the next line.

Length of pause is important in poetry. Stanza pauses which mark the end of a stanza should be longer than the linear or end-of-line pause. The continuity of the stanza must be preserved and over-long pauses should not break it.

Poetry has a balancing pause which is the natural pause within the line. The term CAESURA is sometimes applied to this. A good poetry speaker must use this pause. It gives the lilt and balance to a line and adds considerably to the musical quality, often helping to point the sense. A regularly placed caesural pause can be monotonous and its place in the line is varied in good poetry.

STRESS

Stress is the weight placed on a word when it is spoken to give it emphasis.

WORD STRESS

Luckily those speaking English as their mother-tongue learn which syllables to stress when familiar words are pronounced. The stress on new words has to be learnt.

SENTENCE STRESS

Sense depends to a large extent on the stress being placed on the right syllable and on the right word in a sentence. Nouns and verbs are usually stressed most heavily. Adjectives and adverbs are stressed but to a lesser degree. Placing the stress on the wrong word can alter or at least warp the meaning. Stress should be dictated by the syntax of the sentence. Heavy stressing makes speech laboured and over-emphatic. Words should be made emphatic by the way the voice moves on them and not by sheer weight of utterance. This movement of the voice is

INTONATION

Intonation is the word used to refer to the changes of pitch made by the voice when speaking. It is one of the chief means by which a speaker gives exactness and subtlety of meaning.

The word INFLECTION is also used to refer to pitch changes but is used mostly to refer to the pitch of single words or syllables and so has a narrower application. INTONATION however is used to refer both to the pitch of single words or syllables (whether moving or level) and to the SPEECH TUNES of whole phrases.

A word or phrase may be spoken with any of several different possible intonations each of which will generally convey some difference of meaning or attitude. In practice, intonation (variation of PITCH) is usually combined with other factors which give meaning and colour and individuality to speech: these are variation of VOLUME, TONE and RHYTHM. It is neither possible nor desirable to separate intonation from these other factors. Like intonation they are the natural means of communicating active thought and feeling and are used by every speaker whose voice and speech mechanisms are responsive to intention. The process is largely unconscious.

With all the possible combinations of pitch, volume, tone and rhythm it is not surprising that two equally expert speakers will rarely speak a sentence in exactly the same way. Each will interpret it in a slightly different manner according to his outlook and style and much of these differences will be expressed in intonation.

The intonations used by a speaker are closely connected with (and to some extent an expression of) his habitual thoughts and attitudes. Many people either through lack of sufficiently vital and varied thought or through lack of vocal freedom use a very limited set of intonations both in their own spontaneous speech and (usually more noticeably) in their interpretations of written material. Some knowledge of the nature and functions of basic intonations should help them to become aware of their limitations and to extend the range of meanings they can communicate vocally. However the application to interpretation of consciously-conceived intonations should (if done at all) be done with caution or a mechanical effect will result. If an intonation is not the result of an inner awareness and comprehension of some significance in the words being spoken it will be artificial and the listener will recognize it as such.

It is impossible within the compass of this book to give more than a very brief résumé of the basic facts of English intonation. Much investigation into this has been done in recent years and a list of books is contained in the Bibliography. The following points should be considered:

(a) There are many differences in terminology as used by different writers which may at first be confusing.

(b) The books published are primarily for foreign learners of English and their teachers.

(*c*) The analysis is chiefly concerned with everyday conversational English.

Because of (*b*) and (*c*) students of speech and drama whose native language is English may find the intonations somewhat limited for the interpretation of drama or poetry. They form a useful basis on which to build but in themselves would not achieve subtlety.

THE MARKING OF INTONATION

Instrumental (and therefore objective) analysis of vocal pitch in the speaking of a sentence will show a wavy line rather like the outline of a hilly landscape with gaps where the voiceless sounds occur.

He   says   he   won't   be able   to   mend   it.

A picture such as that drawn above is not very helpful in practical teaching and intonation marking is usually simplified into a system which is more significant. Several different methods are in use but the simplest to draw makes use of a line for every stressed syllable and a dot for every unstressed syllable. Significant pitch changes nearly always occur on stressed syllables and this is clearly indicated by the direction of the line. Stressed syllables do not always have a pitch change and are frequently spoken on a level pitch which is indicated by a level line. The same sentence as shown above, said with the same intonation, would appear thus:

He   says   he   won't   be   able   to   mend   it.

It may be easier to hear an intonation pattern if instead of being spoken it is whistled.

The above falling tune is a basic pattern of unemphatic statement in the English language. A speaker who does not see any significance in a sentence he is speaking will tend to use it. A sequence of sentences said with this tune is bound to be dull since it is merely a series of plain statements unlinked to each other and with no suggestion that there is anything implied but not spoken. On the other hand a persistent refusal to use a falling tune when appropriate because it is thought that a "rising inflection" should be used instead can be equally monotonous and destructive of meaning.

The same sentence said with a rising tune at the end might appear like this:—

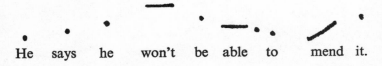

He   says   he   won't   be   able   to   mend   it.

This would have the effect of leaving the matter open; a reply perhaps is invited from the listener or an implication has been made which will be understood by the listener. The exact interpretation would depend on the context. No such invitation or implication is usually conveyed by a falling tune which has the inherent quality of finality.

This sentence could also be spoken with a Fall-Rise intonation on the word "mend". This might imply that he could not repair it but could provide a replacement.

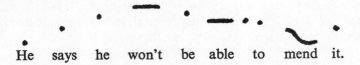

He   says   he   won't   be   able   to   mend   it.

So far only variations on the intonation of the word "mend" have been considered. This is the last stressed syllable of the phrase (or "intonation group") and as such is a key factor in

English intonation. It is generally called the "nucleus". It would be possible to pick out any of the other words in the sentence by means of intonation (in conjunction with stress) and so give the sentence a different meaning. For example the word "says" may be given an emphasis by intonation and stress which would imply doubt in the truth of the man's statement that he couldn't mend it. Or the second "he" might be emphasised by intonation and stress so as to give the meaning that HE wouldn't be able to mend it but someone else might. And so on.

It may be useful to be able to recognize and reproduce for oneself the following set of intonations. (It must not be thought that they represent the full range of possibilities.)

Some possible meanings (depending on context).

1. Low Fall   Yes \   Definite affirmative but no enthusiasm. Possibly rather grim.

2. High Fall   Yes \   More emphatic; possibly enthusiastic.

3. Low Rise   Yes ⌐   Might be said in answering the telephone or casually to your own name or in agreeing with what someone has said so far.

4. High Rise   Yes /   Rather surprised or animated.

5. Low Fall-Rise   Yes ⌐   Affirmative with some implication; it could be slight doubt or an invitation to continue.

6. High Fall-Rise Yes \⌐ Strong affirmative with an implication; possibly "I've told you so a dozen times already."

7. Rise-Fall   Yes ⌐\ Meaning perhaps "most certainly" or "I should think so, too!"

8. Level   Yes —   This hardly exists in English as a complete intonation group but only as a part of a larger pattern nearly always containing a nucleus on which there is a change of

pitch. A nearly level low pitch could possibly be used here to indicate utter boredom.

The above examples are given only as a means of remembering the basic intonations of English. Complicated patterns may be built out of them and the intervening unstressed syllables, when speaking complete sentences. When they are used in speaking a word which is part of a larger intonation pattern the significance they have will depend on the intonations used in the rest of the sentence. Even when a single word such as the "Yes" chosen as an illustration is spoken with a certain intonation the exact significance of that will depend on the context and may indeed be so subtle as to defy exact definition in words.

The analysis of intonation is a highly complex subject and the student of speech and drama may well find his own natural ear and habits aided by the application of a little basic knowledge will be the best means of acquiring the ability to use good intonation.

WORD AND VOCAL PRACTICE

Exercises for the word fall into two parts. The first is concerned with the formation of individual vowels and consonants by the speech organs. These organs have already been exercised during the work on tone. Vowel shapes have been made accurate during the resonator scale practice. In this section the vowel practice has to be extended to include diphthongs. After dealing with consonants individually they can be linked with vowels and sound patterns made.

The second part of word practice is for connected speech. Once the word has been achieved meaning complicates the issue.

DIPHTHONG PRACTICE

When making a diphthong the aim should be a steady continuous movement of the speech organs resulting in a glide. Success depends on the accuracy of the starting position and the correct direction of the glide.

In unstressed positions and in some regional speech they lose their diphthongal quality and become pure vowels.

1. Speak the centring diphthongs rhythmically checking the starting position carefully and experiencing the sensation of movement of the tongue (and lips where applicable)

HERE
HAIR
HOAR
TOUR

2. Speak the closing diphthongs in the same way.

HAY
HIGH
HOW
HOY
HOE

Note the movement of the tongue: the rising of the front for HAY and HIGH but with considerable difference in the length of the glide: the movement from back through centre to front when HOY is said: the lip as well as tongue movement in HOE.

COMMON FAULTS OF DIPHTHONGS

(a) Two sounds are made instead of a glide.
(b) The glide is taken too far with an exaggerated effect.

CONSONANT PRACTICE

The accuracy of consonant formation depends on many factors among them:

(a) The ear.
(b) Muscular dexterity of the speech organs.
(c) Sensory discrimination of the speech organs.
(d) Knowledge of the formation of speech sounds.
(e) Early speech education.

The order of importance of these factors varies with each individual.

Consonant practice is often termed ARTICULATION. In a

strict sense this means the coming together of two speech organs to make a sound. In a wider way it is used to mean the grouping together of vowels and consonants to make connected speech. ENUNCIATION is a better term for this.

EXERCISES FOR INDIVIDUAL CONSONANTS

1. Ease the jaw.
2. EASE
   STRENGTHEN
   MAKE FLEXIBLE
   GAIN CONTROL of the speech organs making the sound. Exercises for this have been described under Exercises for the Speech Organs.
3. Make the sound quietly and accurately. Repeat it slowly increasing rate gradually.
4. Repeat the sound making various rhythms.
   kkk*k* kkk*k* kkk*k*
5. Combine the sound with vowels, varying the position
   kah ahk ahkah
6. Combine the consonant with others in complicated sound patterns.

COMMON FAULTS IN THE ARTICULATION OF INDIVIDUAL SOUNDS

PLOSIVES

Voiced

(*a*) If the sound is over-articulated a short vowel follows the plosion in final position.
(*b*) It should be remembered that voiced plosives in final position are partially devoiced. Over-voicing them disturbs the balance of the enunciation.

Unvoiced

(*a*) Some speakers make a slight fricative instead of a clean plosion. This is known as AFFRICATION.

NASALS

When the speech organs part before vocalization ceases the nasal is "released". This is particularly common in s*ing*. A plosive is often added to this sound in some regional speech.

LATERALS

The tip articulation of dark *l* sometimes causes difficulty. Some people use a short back vowel with lip rounding in place of the true alveolar articulation.

FRICATIVES

(*a*) Too much breath is sometimes used and this is usually combined with weak muscular articulation. The result is an untidy weak sound. Undue length is often added to the fault.

(*b*) the *r* sound suffers from a number of faults. Lack of friction is a common one. A frictionless continuant is substituted for it. Another fault is the use of a lip articulation for the *r* which should be made between the tip of the tongue and the back of the teeth-ridge.

(*c*) *s* has a variety of faults. The most frequent gives the effect of a too low pitched sound; it is near *sh* or *th*. Another fault is a high-pitched "whistly" *s* sound.

(*d*) Inability to differentiate between voiced and voiceless sounds results in *f* being substituted for *v* and *th*in for *th*en.

FLAPPED

Few untrained speakers use flapped *r*. It adds neatness to speech although it should be used with discretion.

FAULTS IN CONNECTED SPEECH

These are too numerous to list but can be grouped thus:

(a) Those due to poor muscular effort resulting in slack weak enunciation.

(b) Over-brisk speech of a jerky type.

(c) Pronunciation faults arising from poor speech education.

(d) Insufficient gradation (sometimes due to a desire to be clear without a teacher's direction).

(e) Lack of balance in the speech due to the use of the wrong phonemic variant.

(f) Undue lengthening of vowels.

(g) No use of the lateral and nasal plosions.

GENERAL PRACTICE FOR THE VOICE

To make the voice a fine flexible instrument final practice must be given in achieving every possible effect with tone and speech. This need not be kept to language but should embrace a range as wide as the apparatus and the imagination allow.

Work should follow these lines:

(a) Tone used as widely as possible to include violent noisy passages, lyrical lines, calling, onomatopoeic effects—from fog-horns to musical instruments.

(b) The use of the voice in a variety of rooms, halls, theatres and through the microphone.

(c) The gaining of dexterity in volume changes.

(d) An increasing of the musical value of the voice by ear training with a piano and other musical instruments and singing. As the range is widened it should be applied in intonation work.

(e) Speech rapidity. This should be increased.

(f) Words should be brought alive and the full range given zest, from the strong dynamic to the delicate.

APPENDIX: ADDITIONAL EXERCISES

Detailed exercises for breath, note, tone and word have been given in the appropriate sections of this book. Material, mostly traditional, for vocal practice and application has been collected in the author's book *Speech Practice* (Pitman). The following ideas and poems may also be useful:

1. Clapping to a rhythm is a way of "warming up" for a voice practice. As the clapped rhythm is established and energy increases, spoken sounds and words can be introduced.

Try this simple rhythm first. One person taps twice with a pencil on a wooden surface, then everyone claps:—

tap tap clap
tap tap clap
tap tap clap
CLAP CLAP CLAP

If a group is taking part, a contra-rhythm can be tried:

CLAP   CLAP   clap-clap
CLAP

2. George MacBeth has written a clapping poem. It is hard work so the first part only is offered here.

Numerical Analysis of "Brazilian Poem" from the German of Friederike May-röcker

(. . . 2 2 6 2 3 6: 2 3 3-6 3 8; 3
6 9 4 8 8; 3 6 10;
9 3 5; 2-2: 5 4 6!
2 10 6 6 (8)—4 3 6 11;
5 6; 8 7; 2 3 6 . . .)
9 5 3 5: 2 3 2
10 4
5 8; 3 9 2 3; 5 3 4 3 3 9 9:(4!)
3 6 3 3 4—9 6; 7
3 3 5; 8; 3 3 6; 10 (3 3 7 4 2 3!)

This looks a puzzle until you realize that each number represents the number of claps to be given. Pause to separate one number from the next. Of course you can use any sound you like instead of, or as well as, claps. Done by a group it has a powerful effect and generates energy besides using it.

3. Another good warming-up ploy is to speak a stanza of a poem as a round. Those with a strongly defined rhythm are best for the purpose. Here is an example by David Bell and Angela Konrad.

There are many ways of playing with this. It falls easily into a four-part arrangement.

> Down by the Mersey
> Playing on a bandstand
> John, Paul, George
> And Ringo Starr

> Started as a skiffle group
> Then made the big time
> Found they could only go
> So far.

Once it has been gone through in parts, it's fun if each individual dodges about using words and lines in any way provided the rhythm is kept.

If four parts are used the ending goes better thus:—
> go so far
>   go so far
>   go so far
>   found they could only go so
>   far

4. A good noisy example can be releasing vocally and emotionally. The two following poems by David Bell follow primitive rhythms.

Try to let the sounds you are making come from the middle of your being and project them far into the distance.

> Call it aloud, aloud, aloud!
> Sing it long, long, long!
> Words and whisper, whip, whine,
>   whip.
> Shout it out, out, out!
> Man sits and speaks, man stands
>   and shouts, man convinces.
> The words live!

5. Another stirring poem by David Bell:—

Besides loudness, you can enjoy a strong, lifting attack on the words.

> *The Gale*
> Twisting me, tearing me,
> The knife cuts hard, the flesh
>   withdraws,

Between torn, tormenting terror,
  gripping
Me, hurting me.

6. You may like to sing an exercise. Peter Kay has arranged this one especially for resonance. It presupposes you have a piano and someone able to read music.

When you can sing it competently, change key.

The guitar is another instrument useful for singing and speaking exercises. The flute, too, blends well with the spoken word.

7. The material that follows is a collection of sound poems by Bob Cobbing. There are no rules to follow when interpreting them and this makes them particularly valuable for engendering vocal flexibility. They can be whispered, intoned, sung or spoken as your inclination and imagination dictate.

There is also freedom in deciding whether they are followed through from beginning to end, or certain lines or words are repeated. If a group is trying them, there is no need for

everyone to be active all the time.
Shape and meaning are increased if the
number speaking at one time varies.
The interpretation should be spontaneous and not dictated or rigidly
prepared.

Cri Zok

Cri zok cri zok cri zok
Rinkle stammen rinkel stammen
Tak tak tak tak
Gros temps gros temps gros
Temps temps temps tempe
Temps terre temps terre
Plume de ma tante
Tu dors tu dors
To two too door
A door adore
Toc toc toc toc
Tu dors tu dors
Zzzzzz Zzzzzz
Z

(From *ABC in Sound*)

This is an easy one to begin
with. Lines can be repeated
but as a 'clock' poem. It is
very satisfactory just going
through from beginning to
end.

8.

Bombast

Bombast bombast
Bomb bomb bomb bast
Bombast
Emphase
Em- em- em- phase
Bombast emphase
Bombast
Phébus

(From *ABC in Sound*)

You have to decide for yourself what the sound poems
'mean'. This has been regarded as a clock poem and as a
bombardment by different
groups working on it. Bob
Cobbing often uses French
words in his poems so check
the pronunciation if you are
not certain of it.

9.

La Lune Loop

Loop
La lune Loop
Ontala ontala tala tala
Low loom Bleep
Bleep la lune Loop
La nuit est morte

La Lune has been considered
to be a study of a dripping tap
but it has also been used as a
comment on interplanetary
travel.

Bleep
La lune Loop
Le jour est mort
Ontala tala tala

La loupe
Tala tala
Les runes Droop
Langage
Est mort

It says something about the death of language in the usual sense and about the birth of a language of sound. It can involve a wide range with high Loops and Bleeps and low ontalas.

(From *ABC in Sound*)

10.   *Naomi*

naomi imean imoan naomi nioma nioma amoin amion
maino maino oniam oniam moina aniom aniom moina
noami imaon imaon noamo niamo niamo omain omain
miano miano onaim onaim moani inaom inaom moani
noima amion amion noima naimo naimo omian omain
miona miona anoim anoim maoni inoam inoam maoni
maoni inoam inoam maoni miona miona anoim anoim
naimo naimo omian omian noima amion amion noima
moani inaom inaom moani miano miano onaim onaim
niamo niamo omain omain noami imaon imaon noami
moina aniom aniom moina maino maino oniam oniam
nioma nioma amoin amoin naomi imoan imoan naomi

Move about as you wish on this poem with emphasis on the nasals and the vowels. If you have a group working on this, the overall word to emerge will probably be the title word NAOMI.

11.   *Ana Perenna*

ana nina na-ana danu una dana
an-anasa nana anu anis ina una
ay mari ramya amarimi rama
enma ira mariamne ariana rana ira
anné ira marienna mirima nana mirim
si tiana ana itis an-athanah tana
hanah-ita ariande ana edna ira ati hanah

an-athanah tana si tiana ana itis
mirima nana mirim anné ira marienna
ariana rana ira enma ira mariamne
amarimi rama ay mari ramya
anu anis ina una an-anasa nana
ana danu una dana ana nina na
(ana danu, una dana, etc)

This one needs delicacy and musicality. You will be surprised at the lyrical achievement that is possible. Each half-line (and the whole poem) is a palindrome and, at the end, it allows for repeats.

12.

Fragment

sasa kassee jo ook arsaka see
joass sackoo jusoo jaa
ajeck sojooka kee reko sooja jaake
aaeouauueeooeauo
okkuakeko jukokkua aeja reekokussa
saarruu oukekoju
raka jee sseee aajakakee jjeaujok
ouaeooeeuuauoeaa
sakasee jo ook arsaka see
joassak koojusoo jaa
ajeck sojooka kee
rekosoo ja jaake
aaeouauueeooeauo
okkua keko
juko kua
aoja
ree

Plenty of vowel work comes into this. Aim at neatness and accuracy. The "j" should be pronounced as English "y".

13.

1

kurrirrurriri

twonk
rol rol rol
twonk twonk
rol rol rol rol
twonk
rol rol rol rol rol
twonk twonk
rol rol rol rol rol rol

Insects or birds are the subject of these studies. Give them full onomatopoeic treatment. Stanza 1 – frog and lark. Stanza 2 – the tse-tse fly and other noxious insects. Stanza 3 – crows and others. Stanza 4 – chickens, cocks and hens. Stanza 5 – doves and pigeons. Stanza 6 – a jaunt-

about song, which may also
be used, whole or in part,
between the other stanzas.

2
bubula bubulela
bamberoo bumb-
   harali
bomboolios bum-
   berooli
tse tse ntsintsi
bumberoo bamb-
   harali
bumboolios bam-
   berooli
tse tse ntsintsi
bomboo bumarali
bubuluza boozuza
bomboloza zezu

3
kah kah cacak-
   djeda
kra kra grika
kra kara kra kacha
kah chacha kah
   graji
khrij khrij
kra grika gra
   chacha
khrij karat khrij
   karot
gra graji grika
   chacha
kra klah kah

4
kokro co rico
koklo quiquiriqui
okoko okoka
kuku kukkata
kukko caracaca
kukuk kaluruk
kukuduna kukukasi
kokro coquelicot
koklo tsu koklo no

5
pip
pipio pigione
pippione piccione
   pipare
pipire pipiare pigio-
   lare pippionare
pippolini pipelni
   pipegni
pipay pipok
pip

6
timpa tampa
tump tup
tumbuk timno
tumbak tamno
timpa tampa
tomp tump
tom tom tump tup
tum tum tomp tump

BIBLIOGRAPHY

INTONATION

1. *Intonation of Colloquial English*, by J. D. O'Connor & G. F. Arnold (Longmans, Green, 1961). Records spoken by the authors are available.
2. *The Groundwork of English Intonation*, by Roger Kingdon (Longmans, Green, 1958).
3. *An English Intonation Reader*, by W. R. Lee (Macmillan, 1960). Records spoken by the author are available.
4. *English Intonation Practice*, by Roger Kingdon (Longmans, Green, 1958).
   (Phonetic transcription is not used in any of the above except as an additional item in No. 3. All the books may be read and understood fully without a knowledge of phonetic notation.)

VOICE AND SPEECH: GENERAL

5. *Cunningham's Text-Book of Anatomy*, edited by Brash (Oxford Medical Publications).
6. *The Respiratory Muscles*, by E. J. Moran Campbell (Lloyd-Luke).
7. *Living Anatomy*, by R. D. Lockhart (Faber).
8. *The Mechanism of the Larynx*, by V. E. Negus (Heinemann).

PRONUNCIATION

9. *An English Pronouncing Dictionary*, by Daniel Jones (Dent).
10. *Chamber's Twentieth Century Dictionary* (Chambers).
11. *The Shorter Oxford English Dictionary*, (2 vols), (Oxford University Press).
12. *An Introduction to the Pronunciation of English*, by A. C. Gimson (Edward Arnold, 1962).

ALEXANDER TECHNIQUE

13. *The Alexander Principle*, by Wilfred Barlow (Victor Gollancz, 1973).